First World War
and Army of Occupation
War Diary
France, Belgium and Germany

55 DIVISION
165 Infantry Brigade,
Brigade Trench Mortar Battery
2 June 1916 - 20 July 1916

WO95/2927/4

The Naval & Military Press Ltd
www.nmarchive.com
Published in association with The National Archives

Published by

The Naval & Military Press Ltd

Unit 10 Ridgewood Industrial Park,

Uckfield, East Sussex,

TN22 5QE England

Tel: +44 (0) 1825 749494

www.naval-military-press.com

www.nmarchive.com

This diary has been reprinted in facsimile from the original. Any imperfections are inevitably reproduced and the quality may fall short of modern type and cartographic standards.

© Crown Copyright
Images reproduced by permission of The National Archives, London, England, 2015.

Contents

Document type	Place/Title	Date From	Date To
Heading	Trench Mortar Batt		
Heading	55th Division 165th Infy Bde Trench Mortar Btts. 1916 May-Aug 1916		
War Diary	War Diary for May 1916 of 165/2 Trench Mortar Battery		
War Diary	Wailly Sector	02/06/1916	28/06/1916
Heading	War Diary Of The 165th Trench Mortar Battery For The Period 1st August To 31st August 1916 Vol 4		
War Diary	Ref. Map Guillemont	01/08/1916	30/08/1916
Heading	War Diary Of 165th Machine Gun Company For Period December 1st-31st 1916. Vol XI		
War Diary	In The Field	01/12/1916	31/12/1916
Heading	165th Brigade 55th Division 165th Light Trench Mortar Battery July 1916		
Heading	War Diary Of The 165th Trench Mortar Battery 55th (West Lancashire) Division For The Period 1st July 1916 To 31st July 1916. Vol 3		
War Diary	Wailly Sector	01/07/1916	20/07/1916

TRENCH MORTAR BATT.

55TH DIVISION
165TH INFY BDE

TRENCH MORTAR BTTS.
1916 MAY ~~JUN~~ - AUG 1916.

Army Form C. 2118.

LV TM

WAR DIARY for May 1916

INTELLIGENCE SUMMARY of 165/2 Trench Mortar Battery (3" Stokes).

Vol 1

Place	Date	Hour	Summary of Events and Information	Remarks and references to Appendices
			This Battery was formed on April 14th, and, after 7 days training at the Third Army Trench Mortar School, came into the Wailly Sector on the 22nd of April. The Battery was composed of men drawn from the 6th and 7th Kings L'pool Regt, and was placed under the command of Lieut. E. Henshell of the 6th Kings L'pool Regt. The Battery took over the right sector of the 165th Brigade Sector, and was for some weeks mainly occupied in constructing fresh offensive positions in the line. Previous to this the 166/1 Trench Mortar Battery (3" Stokes) had covered the entire front of the 165th Brigade. The Battery fired for the first time on the 28th April. On May 12th Lt Henshell was recalled to his battalion and the command of the Battery devolved upon 2nd Lieut	

Army Form C. 2118.

WAR DIARY for May 1916
or
INTELLIGENCE SUMMARY 166/2 Trench Mortar Battery
(Erase heading not required.)

Instructions regarding War Diaries and Intelligence Summaries are contained in F. S. Regs., Part II. and the Staff Manual respectively. Title Pages will be prepared in manuscript.

Place	Date	Hour	Summary of Events and Information	Remarks and references to Appendices
			Robertson of the 7th Kings L'pool Regt. On Saturday May 22nd the Battery, acting in concert with the 166/1 Trench Mortar Battery, arranged to put up a barrage for a raiding party of the 7th L'pools. This raid was however postponed. On May 27th 2nd Lieut W. H. Davidson of the 6th Kings L'pool Regt joined the Battery. During the month of May the Battery fired 61 rounds, mainly on enemy sap. heads in its own section of the Brigade front.

A. J. Robertson 2/Lt
OC 166/2 Trench Mortar Battery. | |

WAR DIARY or INTELLIGENCE SUMMARY

Army Form C. 2118.

4/1, 6.5/2 Trench Mortar Battery

for June 1916.

Place	Date	Hour	Summary of Events and Information	Remarks and references to Appendices
Neuilly Sector	2.6.16	5 pm	2 Lt W.H.H. Davidson took over command of the Battery on the 27th May 1916.	
	4.6.16	4.56 am	Registering on enemy front line trench about R.29.d.2.6. 11 shells fired. Used Very #satisfactory. Bombardment + barrage to assist of raiding party of 5th the Kings. Bombay Fused R.F., who proposed to enter the trenches at R.29.d.55. Enemy bombardment shelling flat. had badly (could observe it) had the bombardment falling left of the Our fire was not observed, but all guns were fired well left of the party. It seems it occurred on the infantrymate occurrence. 132 shells fired.	
	6.6.16	6 pm	Ct infantry's request S.A.C (R.29 + 9.6) was shelled. 13 rounds fired. 2 duds satisfactory.	
	7.6.16		Registration on S.A.P (R.30.a.2.8) 3 shells satisfactory	
	8.6.16		Registration of Sh. at R.29.78.40. 6 shells satisfactory	
	13.6.16		In conjunction with /SS T.M Bttf. Retaliation + searching of enemy mortar. 18 shells satisfactory	
Neuilly S	15.6.16		at enemy's request S.A.P at R.14.C.77 was shelled. 35 shells satisfactory	

Army Form C. 2118.

WAR DIARY to June 1916
or
INTELLIGENCE SUMMARY   ₤ 165/2 T.M. Batty

(Erase heading not required.)

Instructions regarding War Diaries and Intelligence Summaries are contained in F. S. Regs., Part II. and the Staff Manual respectively. Title Pages will be prepared in manuscript.

Place	Date	Hour	Summary of Events and Information	Remarks and references to Appendices
Woolly Switch	17.6.16		Sub M19 c 7.9. 11 rounds 1 dud. Satisfactory.	
	18.6.16		Retaliation on enemy trench mortar. Bombarded with Y55 T.n.B. 10 rounds fired. Bombardt. short of enemy mortar. Req.d. 79. Enemy mortar did not fire for 36 hours afterwards.	
	18.6.16		Sub M19 c 79. Infantry report 2 rounds fired Satisfactory at report, infantry. 10 shells fired at sub B. (R29 c 91) Very satisfactory. 1 dud.	
	19.6.16		Sub M19 c 79. Satisfactory 5 shells fired	
	19.6.16	Battery moved to new pos.	Sub M19 c 79. Infantry report 25 shells were fired at sub M19 c 2-3. At Battalion commanders request. 2 duds. Satisfactory	
	20.6.16		165/1 + 165/2 become numbers 1 Section + 2 section of 165 T.M. Battery. As 165/1 is at present armed with 3.7" trench mortars, nobody has been attached to command the 165 T.M. Battery.	
	20.6.16		9 rounds fired in enemy trench between R29 & 85 — retaliation. Stand satisfactory.	

Army Form C. 2118.

WAR DIARY or INTELLIGENCE SUMMARY

June 1916. (165/T.M. Battery)

(Erase heading not required.)

Instructions regarding War Diaries and Intelligence Summaries are contained in F. S. Regs., Part II. and the Staff Manual respectively. Title Pages will be prepared in manuscript.

Place	Date	Hour	Summary of Events and Information	Remarks and references to Appendices
Kelly	25/6/16	4pm	In accordance with instructions contained by the 55th Division the Battery bombarded an zone from Sq 9 & 1 to Sq 9 2.6. 570 shells fired during a 30 minutes bombardment. Very satisfactory	
	26/6/16	11am	160 shells fired	
	27/6/16	6am	240 shells fired	
	28/6/16	5.30am	48 shells fired	
	29/6/16	5.55pm	600 shells fired one general trench. The whole function was very successful - the Battery had only 5 (2) men slightly wounded. Ammunition supply was the most difficult matter.	
			During the month the Battery has fired 1706 rounds of which 8 are known to have been duds.	

W.H.D. Andrew
2/Lt
O/c 165/T.M. Battery

165 Tm Bty
Vol 4

War Diary
of the
165th Trench Mortar Battery
for the period
1st August to 31st August
1916.

Army Form C. 2118.

WAR DIARY
INTELLIGENCE SUMMARY

165 Trench Mortar Battery

(Erase heading not required.)

Place	Date	Hour	Summary of Events and Information	Remarks and references to Appendices
Pt. Map GUILLEMONT.	1/8/16 to 6/8/16	—	The Battery marched by stages in accordance with situation orders into the line relieving the 166 T.M.Bty on the night of August 6th 1916.	
	7/8/16	—	2 Guns were placed in position in COCHRANE ALLEY.	
	8/8/16	—	4 Guns were placed in position - 2 at the BARRIER and 2 in JACKSON ST.	
	"	—	All attachments prepared for action during attack by the Infantry but there was no firing	
	"	—	2/Lt W.H.H. DAVIDSON was wounded - the Command of the Battery passing to 2/Lt. F.O. NORTON.	
	9/8/16	—	367 Rounds were fired from the 2 guns in the BARRIER on enemy's BARRIER 4 trenches in the vicinity in support of Infantry attack.	
	10/8/16	—	The 2 guns in COCHRANE ALLEY registered enemy Strong Point & M.G. emplacement, firing 10 rounds.	
		—	The 2 guns at the BARRIER fired 367 rounds "barrage" fire in support of Infantry attack.	

Army Form C. 2118.

WAR DIARY
INTELLIGENCE SUMMARY
(Erase heading not required.)

Place	Date	Hour	Summary of Events and Information	Remarks and references to Appendices
			165 Trench Mortar Battery. Sheet 2.	
	11/8/16	—	196 rounds were fired from the 2 guns in COCHRANE ALLEY on enemy Strong Point into RAVINE in support of Infantry Attack	
	"	—	The 2 guns at the BARRIER fired 94 rounds in conjunction with the Artillery who were bombarding enemy's trenches & Strongpost near enemy BARRIER Trenches in the vicinity	
	12/8/16	—	The Battery was relieved by the 166 T.M. Btty & marched back to Bivouac area on the morning of the 13th.	
	14/9/16	—	In accordance with operation order the Battery marched from Bivouac area to Ville-Sur-Ancre.	
	19/8/16	—	Entrained at MERICOURT for MARTAINEVILLE & marched into billets at CERISY.	
	30/9/16	—	Moved by rail in accordance with operation orders	

G.O.Paxton 2/Lieut.
O/c 165 T.M. Btty

CONFIDENTIAL

Vol II

War Diary
of
165th Machine Gun Company
for period
December 1st – 31st 1916

WAR DIARY or INTELLIGENCE SUMMARY

Army Form C. 2118

Instructions regarding War Diaries and Intelligence Summaries are contained in F.S. Regs, Part II. and the Staff Manual respectively. Title Pages will be prepared in manuscript.

(Erase heading not required.)

Place	Date	Hour	Summary of Events and Information	Remarks and references to Appendices
In the Field	1/12/16		Indirect fire cancelled until further orders. Heavy bombardment on our left with slight shelling on our right.	
	2/12/16		Enemy Quiet. Orders issued re S.O.S. signals by adjoining Battalions.	
	3/12/16		Enemy French Mortars fire in district of RAILWAY WOOD. G.S. emplacement cleared & made useable again.	
	4/12/16		Enemy Quiet. Slight day. Disjunction of positions in rear for a further Troupe.	
	5/12/16		Enemy Quiet. New emplacement built at HELL FIRE CORNER	
	6/12/16		Enemy Quiet. New emplacement in BEEK TRENCH finished	
	7/12/16	P.M.	Relieved by 164 M.G. Coy and proceeded to huts at BRANDHOEK	
	7/12/16 to 17/12/16		Company in huts at BRANDHOEK — Rest & Training	
	17/12/16	P.M.	Relieved 164 M.G. Coy in the line	
	18/12/16		Slight activity in front of enemy Artillery. Several clearing up of dug outs & emplacement, S.A.A. etc.	
	19/12/16		Enemy still retaliated active. Slight snowfall	
	20/12/16		Artillery activity - quiet on both sides. Some damage done to PICADILLY and CAMBRIDGE trenches	
	21/12/16		Continued artillery activity. Another damage to drive trenches, also GULLY TRENCH. Drifts snowy	
	22/12/16		Heavy shelling from both sides still carried on. Brigade on our left made a raid on enemy trenches	
	27/12/16		Night of 26/27 Blown to bits. Indirect fire scheme continued from where broken off	
			Artillery Mine-Waters much quieter. Considerable aeroplane activity.	
	24/12/16		Weather dull and black. Own artillery active	
	25/12/16		Weather showery. Evening very slight activity with artillery	
	26/12/16		Weather frosty and fair. Intermittent shelling on both sides	
	27/12/16		Two adjacent positions changed we with the front line. Enemy Artillery and French Artillery active. Weather fair	
	28/12/16		Enemy Artillery active. Our artillery replied vigorously	
	29/12/16		Weather dull. Snow and Westerns very active but Section of our Bn. M.G. Coy in with new man for instruction.	
	30/12/16		Weather fine. Instruction going. No 3 gun in 4 section officers uninstructed. Quiet day	
	31/12/16		Enemy Artillery active with trench kopy mine guns. District of YPRES and ECOLE Welsh mine than usual	

Stuart-Orford 2/Lt.
for O.C. 16th Wilts Machine Gun Company

165th Brigade.

55th Division.

165th LIGHT TRENCH MORTAR BATTERY

JULY 1916

War Diary
of the
165th Trench Mortar Battery.
55th (West Lancashire) Division
for the period
1st July, 1916 to 31st July, 1916.

Army Form C.2118.

WAR DIARY
or
INTELLIGENCE SUMMARY
(Erase heading not required.)

165 Trench Mortar Battery
July 1916.

Instructions regarding War Diaries and Intelligence Summaries are contained in F.S. Regs., Part II. and the Staff Manual respectively. Title Pages will be prepared in manuscript.

Place	Date	Hour	Summary of Events and Information	Remarks and references to Appendices
Wailly Sector.	1/7/16	7.20 AM	Last day of operations. The Battery fired 251 rounds on enemys trenches (Arrastan trns) with good effect.	
"	7/7/16		No 1 Section proceeded to Trench Mortar School for re armament with 3" Stokes Mortars	
"	13/7/16		460 rounds fired in connection with Smoke barrage in accordance with operation orders.	
"	14/7/16		No 1 Section returned from Trench Mortar School with 3" Stokes Mortars	
"	16/7/16	12.15 A.M.	Battery opened fire at 12.15 A.M. on R.29.@.79.39 (Sp.Y) enemys trenches. Communication trenches in accordance with operation orders. 200 rounds expended.	
"	16/7/16		20 rounds fired on R.29.d.75.25 (Sp.F) at Coy Commanders request with satisfactory results.	
"	17/7/16		20 rounds fired on M.19.d.2.5 (Sp.G.1) at Coy Commanders request in conjunction with the Artillery - Result satisfactory.	
"	20/7/16		Left Wailly Sector. Embodied with D Division.	

W.H. Davidson Lt
O/C 165 T.M.B